THE ANXIETY VIRUS
*Three Essential Strategies to Build Immunity
to Uncertainty in the COVID Crisis*

By Jennifer Shannon, LMFT
With Doug Shannon

Monkey Mind Books

ISBN 978-0-578-69399-6

Table of Contents

1. Uncertainty

Imagine the headline:

ANXIETY CURVE STILL RISING

Maybe you've always been susceptible to anxiety, or maybe you thought yourself immune. Either way, by now we've all caught the "Anxiety virus."

Like homebound agoraphobics, we long to be out in the world, but home is the only place we feel safe. We wash our hands constantly but still doubt that we're germ-free, like those with contamination OCD. We scan our bodies looking for symptoms of illness as if we were suffering from hypochondria. We don't just buy groceries, we panic-shop. We agonize over absent loved ones as if we had separation anxiety. And the tension between us in the streets is palpable, as if we were all suffering from social anxiety.

Health: Are my elderly parents safe? Are these body sensations signs of Covid-19? Dare I go back to work?

Finances: Is my job safe? Will government aid be available? How safe are my investments?

Supplies: Toilet paper, flour, rice, medications, meat—will there be enough?

Social: Should I wear a mask? Is it safe to go to the mall or a restaurant? If I shelter in place too long, will I lose my friends?

General: Will there be a second surge? Will my children fall behind academically? Do our elected officials know what they're doing?

It is true, there is so much more to be anxious about today. But unlike Covid-19, the "Anxiety virus" is not a *novel* strain. It's the same dis-ease we have always struggled with, caused by an underlying condition so widespread that most of us haven't recognized it. Until now. The condition is *intolerance of uncertainty* -- the inability to accept our lack of complete control over our safety and well-being. We are at war with the inherent uncertainty of life, a war that ironically, we can only win if we surrender.

What makes this book so exciting for me to write and share with you is that times of great uncertainty, painful as they are, are our best opportunities to learn how to handle uncertainty. The more we can tolerate being unable to control what happens next, the more relaxed, self-composed and present we

We are at war with the inherent uncertainty of life, a war that ironically, we can only win if we surrender.

can be, allowing for more flexibility and creativity, more wisdom and patience, and more compassion for ourselves and others. These are the qualities that will serve us through this crisis, and the qualities that will enrich us for the rest of our lives.

Right now, right in the middle of the end of the world as we know it, is the perfect moment for us to immunize ourselves to uncertainty and beat the Anxiety virus, and this book will show you exactly how. As a first step, let's shine some light on the source of anxiety, the unconscious part of our brain that strictly enforces our need to be certain.

A failed strategy

Remember the last time you got cut off in traffic? You hit your brakes and swerved before you realized what you'd done. That was the work of your limbic system, a small cluster of brain matter located at the base of your skull, whose sole purpose is to ensure our survival. When the limbic system perceives a threat to our well-being, it sends a fight-or-flight message throughout our nervous system, compelling us to take immediate action to neutralize or avoid the threat.

With so many emerging threats to our health, finances, social connections and food supplies, our limbic system is working overtime. And since it reacts to every tickle in the throat or drop in the stock market with the same blunt instrument it used when that car cut into our lane, our nervous system is getting an overload of fight-or-flight alarms, and not enough rest-and-digest. We can't focus, we can't sleep, and we can't relax.

Our limbic system, hard-wired into our unconscious, is beyond our direct control. It's the oldest part of our brain, and it's been leaping from one uncertainty to the next, like a monkey in the trees, for many thousands of years.

We can't reason with this primal part of ourselves. Your limbic system is yours, but it isn't *You*. It has a mind of its own, a *monkey mind*. We can think of fight-or-flight alarms as the monkey's howling

Woo-woo-woo! DO Something!! Until certainty is achieved, it just won't shut up.

So what do we do to quiet our limbic system? Many of us are aggressively stocking up on food and supplies, constantly checking on the news and on loved ones, and worrying— *lots* of worrying! To our limbic system, these behaviors qualify as "doing something" to eliminate uncertainty, and at least in the short term they can give us some relief. As strategies, though, they fail, because in the long term these behaviors get us more fight-or-flight and anxiety. Panic-shopping, compulsive checking and worrying are *certainty-seeking strategies*. They confirm the limbic system's bias for certainty. Or as I like to say, they "feed the monkey".

In the next chapter, I will show you how we can feed *ourselves* instead, by using strategies that both acknowledge the uncertainty that exists, and enable us to live with it. I'll give you clear instructions on how to change the way you think, act and feel about the things you can't control.

In chapters three and four, we'll break down some common situations that provoke anxiety and see how we can transform them using the strategies from chapter two. Chapters five through eleven are practice situations with step-by-step guidance to help you build immunity faster.

During this COVID crisis, no matter how hard we try to nail down everything safe and tight, there will always be something scary we can't control or that we don't see coming. We cannot reclaim our peace of mind by following the failed strategies of the past, that keep us in a constant state of tension and alert.

We need strategies that condition our limbic system to be less reactive to uncertainty, so we can feel less like fighting or fleeing and more like resting and digesting—even with the uncertainties of a pandemic and worldwide economic recession. The monkey can be trained to sit

quietly on a branch and trust that what we're doing to keep ourselves healthy and financially secure is enough—even when we can't be certain that it is.

2. The Three Strategies

A friend of mine told me what happened to her on a recent trip to the supermarket. As she approached the paper supplies section she saw that there was only one package of toilet paper left on the shelf. Just as she pushed her cart up to it, another shopper darted in front of her and snatched it. My friend was so frustrated that she impulsively bought an armload of paper towels she didn't need. Foolish as she knew she was being, it gave her some relief. I know we can all feel some empathy for my friend; we've all got a limbic system.

Picture yourself on a shopping trip in your favorite supermarket, with your limbic system—represented by a monkey—seated in your shopping cart. You're pushing the cart down the paper supplies aisle and the shelves are empty save for one lone package of toilet paper. You have sufficient toilet paper at home, but you never know when supplies may disappear. And you can see other shoppers approaching. Imagine the conversation you have.

Limbic fight-or-flight message: *Woo-woo-woo! What if you run out?*

You grab the pack and throw it into your cart: *Thanks for the heads up!*

The limbic perception was that, even though you have enough toilet paper, to be certain you won't run out you'll need to have more. You confirmed that perception by taking the toilet paper. This confirmation is like giving a banana to the monkey mind. Just as a child, when "rewarded" with candy for acting out, is more likely to cry next visit to the supermarket, so is the monkey, if rewarded, more likely to sound fight-or-flight alarms the next time you see shelves less than full of toilet paper. The monkey's lesson was, *Howling alarms about toilet paper keeps us certain we are safe.*

This type of exchange between you and your limbic system feeds a cycle of anxiety, and a "monkey mind-set" that is fixed on the pursuit of certainty. We cannot rest unless we are certain we are safe, that we won't get sick, that our job will be secure, that the bills will be paid, that we'll be able to be with our children in a world that we recognize as normal again. If we allow the monkey to stay in charge, dictating our every move with fight-or-flight instructions, we'll never get any rest. We will continue to obsess about the unknowns in our future, compulsively trying to turn them into safe, predictable outcomes.

The one-dimensional monkey mind strategy of attempting to eliminate all uncertainty doesn't work in the world of limitless uncertainty we're living in now. If we can acclimate to uncertainty it won't keep making us sick. I'm going to show you how to build immunity to uncertainty using three new strategies -- one cognitive, one behavioral and one emotional. I call them expansive strategies because, rather than habitually contracting around uncertainty, they intentionally expand around it, allowing space for what we cannot know or control.

Contraction strategy   Expansive strategy

These strategies are based on my decades of Cognitive-Behavioral Therapy (CBT) work with clients who suffer from heightened anxiety — people just like you and me, who only want a little peace.

Strategy #1 Set an Intention

I wanted to make a vegetable soup today, but we were out of vegetables. As I contemplated going to the grocery store, I mentally reviewed all the precautions I'd need to take: wear a mask, bring hand sanitizer, keep a social distance from other shoppers, sanitize everything inside and out when I got home. But I'd just read that the coronavirus can linger in the air in aerosol form. Since I can't be certain my facemasks would protect me from those floating microbes, is it reasonable to breathe?

Safe or not, breathe we must. Our first strategy is to set an intention: to accept that it is OK to stop troubleshooting about things that are beyond our control. Our mantra will be, *I'll do what's reasonable, then accept the uncertainty that's left.* This intention will set the stage for relaxation even when we are uncertain. We will be healthier physically and mentally, and able to think with more focus and clarity, which we need more than ever in a crisis.

Our mantra will be, I'll do what's reasonable, then accept the uncertainty that's left.

Creating this intention is known in Cognitive Behavioral Therapy as *cognitive restructuring*. But as we have probably learned from making positive affirmations and promises to ourselves in the past, we cannot tear down and rebuild our beliefs like Lego block constructions -- especially the unconscious belief that we shouldn't stop worrying until we feel safe. To make our new intention stick, we must practice acting on it as well.

Strategy #2 Curb the Urge

A few weeks after the pandemic reached public consciousness here in the United States, I got an e-mail from a former client I'd treated for health anxiety who was having trouble. "I'm so afraid of getting the Coronavirus, I'm falling back into my old behavior," he wrote. He is a very bright, successful professional who fully understood that his random minor chest pains and scratchy throat, unless they persisted, were unlikely to be signs of contagion. But he wasn't able to wait to see if they persisted. Whenever a potential symptom appeared, he was booking a Zoom session with his doctor.

Every time my client scanned his body for possible symptoms, or consulted his doctor to be reassured, he was reinforcing his limbic system's unquenchable thirst for certainty, conditioning it to be more and more reactive to random sensations. We can't be comfortable with uncertainty when our limbic system is dead set against it. So long

11

as we continue to behave as though certainty is possible, we'll never believe that uncertainty is acceptable.

We can learn to recognize certainty-seeking behaviors by the urgency we feel. Urgency is the calling card of the monkey mind, *Woo-woo-woo! DO something!!* Unless there is an imminent threat that is within our control to prevent, we can choose how to respond.

Not acting on an urge will of course create a different experience for us. When my client resolved not to call his doctor for a day, and followed through with it, he got to experience <u>not</u> being reassured, which was very uncomfortable. Our limbic system doesn't close shop when we ignore its alarms. The monkey will howl twice as loudly and our urges will feel even more urgent. This brings us to our third strategy, what to do instead of giving in.

Strategy #3 Let Fear Metabolize

A few months ago, before social distancing, I met a friend whom I hadn't seen for years, for a drink. I ordered a martini. After a pleasant hour of catching up on all we'd been through it was time to go, but when I stood up I felt so unsteady I sat right back down again. The drink was mixed a good deal stronger than I had expected, and even though I lived only a mile away, I called my husband to come pick me up. It took another full hour for the alcohol to metabolize and to feel normal again.

We'd never order it at a bar, but fear is like a strong martini in one very important way. The active ingredients in the fight-or-flight response -- adrenaline, testosterone and cortisol to name a few -- are organic compounds with specific effects, just like alcohol or any other drug has its effects. The effect of alcohol stays with us for as long it takes the alcohol to metabolize in our bodies. Fear is the same; until it metabolizes, its effects will remain with us and cannot be wished away. Remember, your pounding heart, queasy stomach, sweaty hands and shaky nerves after that close call in traffic? After that fight-or-flight response is triggered, it takes time before we feel normal again.

We understand this about ourselves when we have scares like a near miss in traffic. We show self-compassion by taking deep breaths and perhaps giving a prayer of thanks. We're grateful that our bodies mobilized us to react so quickly, hitting the brake or turning the wheel to avoid a collision.

But we have a far more difficult time accepting and allowing sensations of fear when we're dealing with prolonged, multi-faceted threats like the possibility of getting sick or experiencing financial loss. We don't want to wait for our fear to metabolize; we see no end to it. We try to distract or medicate ourselves to make it go away.

Our third expansive strategy is designed to metabolize the fight-or-flight response in the most efficient way, without making any effort to make it go away. Just as we make space in our minds for uncertain thoughts, we will make space in our bodies for the fear that accompanies uncertainty.

Contracting around emotion

Fear is compounded when we tense ourselves against it. So rather than tightening our stomachs, hunching our shoulders, clenching our fists, and gritting our teeth — what we might call white-knuckling our way through the sensations — with this strategy we do pretty much the opposite.

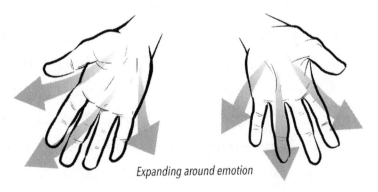

Expanding around emotion

We deliberately relax our belly, lift our head, tuck in our chin, drop our shoulders, open our hands, and loosen our jaw. We follow our breath deep down into our belly, pause, then follow it out with our exhale. This posture creates a dramatic reversal in our musculature; muscles that have been contracted and tense in the belly or chest can expand and relax.

As our muscles relax, we begin to experience an inner space, occupying our bodies in a more intimate way than we are accustomed to. The focus of our awareness drops from our heads into our hearts. Whatever sensations we encounter in this expanded inner space are

Just as we make space in our minds for uncertain thoughts, we will make space in our bodies for the fear that accompanies uncertainty.

welcomed without judgment or attachment. With each mindful breath, our body language says, *I welcome whatever I am feeling.*

Allowing yourself to fully experience negative emotions, like fear, can feel unfamiliar and wrong, especially if you've been clamping down on them for a long time. Emotions from past experiences can get reactivated. If that happens, don't resist them or retell the story that sparked these emotions; that will only trigger more. All we need do is keep opening our physical body and allow it to express what it needs to express. Our bodies know how to metabolize emotions, just as they know how to metabolize food and drink. All we need do is trust the process.

To help you practice this expansive emotional strategy, download my *Turn Fear Into Love* guided meditation at monkeymindbooks.com.

While allowing negative emotions to metabolize can be painful, the rewards are great. The space we create for fight-and-flight to play itself out is the same space that rest-and-digest plays in. As we increase our capacity to handle pain, we simultaneously increase our capacity for pleasure. The more we can welcome fear, the more we will be able to welcome joy.

In the next chapter, we'll look at the uncertainty in some familiar scenarios, and how our strategic choices can influence our limbic system's reaction to them, either for better or worse. And as we will discover, the biggest benefit of learning to tolerate uncertainty is not simply having less anxiety; it's how we can unleash the very skills we need to survive in a crisis. Read on and see how this works!

3. From Hijacked to Handling It

Let's replay our supermarket scene from the first chapter, with the same package of toilet paper on an otherwise empty shelf, but this time using our three expansive strategies.

Limbic fight-or-flight message: *What if you run out? Woo-woo-woo!*

In this scenario, you create an intention to accept the uncertainty about the future availability of toilet paper (Strategy #1). The supply chain and others' hoarding are beyond your control, so you've made an executive decision to accept this uncertainty. So...

You keep walking: *We don't need certainty about toilet paper.*

With your small change of behavior, you're conditioning your limbic system to accept the possibility of running out (Strategy #2). The feeling of potential loss and helplessness this brings up may be strong, but rather than resist this feeling, you open to it, giving it time and space in your body to metabolize (Strategy #3). You take a few long, slow, deep breaths to ground yourself and continue with your shopping. The monkey may not be a bright student, but with enough repetitions of this training it will learn the lesson, and you will break the cycle. You will feel less anxious about your uncertain supply of toilet paper, as well as other supply chain uncertainties. You've gone from being hijacked to handling it!

Stockpiling flexibility

But can we handle it? Curbing the urge to stockpile food and supplies has risks. In a crisis like this, either due to disruption of supply chains or others' hoarding, you very well might run out of something and need to come up with a creative solution. But as I found this out early in the crisis, when I had to mix my own batch of hand sanitizer using a recipe I found on the internet, we *can* handle it! And the positive human qualities that are unlocked when we do handle shortages are a bigger, more durable prize than the short-term relief from anxiety we wanted. Here's another example.

A few days ago, my client Jill told me how disappointed she was that they were out of flour at her favorite supermarket. She wanted to make chocolate chip cookies with her now home-schooled daughters, so she decided to go to another store. Once again she found shelves empty of flour. Shoulders tensed, stomach clenched, she headed to a third supermarket. Once again, no white flour, no whole wheat flour, no any kind of flour. She ended up feeling defeated, anxious and helpless. Jill unnecessarily exposed herself to three different public spaces, which in retrospect, didn't seem very wise, and she wondered if she'd ever be able to bake with her children again.

For Jill, not having access to flour was a great opportunity to practice being flexible. I suggested that she and her children make a "flexibility jar" that they could fill with a marble every time one of them thought of a solution to a shortage. When they met the goal of ten marbles in the jar, they could have an ice cream party to celebrate their flexibility. She loved the idea. When she and her girls decided to make rice crispy treats instead of cookies, they put their first marble in the jar.

When we reframe a shortage as an opportunity, we open and expand instead of contracting. In that open and expanded state we can be more flexible, creative, and composed — the qualities we need to cope with shortages. Confidence that we can handle the uncertainties we face is what allows us to relax in these uncertain times. And looking forward toward an uncertain future, where everything we take for granted could change or disappear, which would you rather have a huge stockpile of flour … or flexibility? Extra toilet paper…. or creativity?

Check in with yourself, not the news

My client was healthy, happily married, and had a job he could do from home, but he was having headaches, stomach pains, difficulty concentrating and he wasn't sleeping well at night. "So many people have it worse off than me, I feel guilty," he told me. "But I'm still scared. I feel like the whole world's gone crazy and life will never be the same."

During our conversation, it became apparent that he was extraordinarily well informed about the coronavirus and the economy. When I asked him how often he checked the news, it turned out that between newspapers, cable news, and the news apps on his phone, he was checking many dozens of times, adding up to as much as six hours a day.

Compulsive checking on news feeds keeps us informed, but it also keeps us agitated. An urgent need to know is a sure sign that our limbic system is engaged. Urgency is characteristic of fight-or-flight alarms. It's the monkey's call to action, *Woo-woo-woo! Find out NOW!!* Before we are aware of it, we're hijacked, and grabbing for our phones.

Getting a quick headline fix may ease our uncertainty discomfort, but it also confirms that uncertainty is dangerous and feeds the monkey. It encourages future interruptions to our work and play, and undermines our ability to focus on our own personal experience in the moment. We must ask ourselves, which is more important to have in life – certainty about what happened there and then? … or the ability to focus and cope in the here and now?

Every time my client felt the urge to check the news was an opportunity to condition his limbic system to be less reactive to uncertainty. When he curbed the urge to check, he was training the monkey that, *Not knowing the very latest news is no cause for alarm.*
Repeating this message, and acting accordingly, is the only way we can get fewer urges to check whatever we've been checking compulsively.

Like my client, you may be checking your temperature compulsively, or closely monitoring your body for symptoms of the coronavirus and calling your doctor. You may be nervously checking on distant loved ones, adult children, or elderly parents, calling or texting them to make sure they're healthy. If we need to check to be certain of anything before we can relax, our relaxation is always conditional until the next uncertainty that comes our way. And uncertainties just keep on coming, don't they?

Next time you feel the anxious urge to check on something, check in with yourself first. Is your anxiety a reliable signal that action is necessary? Or is your limbic system being overactive? Is your need to know time-sensitive, or could it wait?

For example, if you're a chronic temperature checker, you can choose to practice courage by taking your temperature only if you have other persistent symptoms such as a sore throat or a cough. If you're a news feed checker, you may decide to exercise patience and check the news only at pre-established times, such as once in the morning and once in the evening. When we set parameters for our checking behaviors, we are showing the monkey mind who's in charge and signaling that fear won't be driving our behavior.

Yes, there is a short-term reward for taking our temperature, checking our retirement funds, texting the kids or turning on the news whenever we feel uncertain. We get a little certainty. But which do you want during an extended period of crisis -- to know what's going on at a single moment in time ... or to know that you can stay present in any moment, without certainty of what's going on?

Handling any outcome

My client, a software engineer working from home, was for the moment in good financial shape despite the coronavirus. But she was the most recent hire at her company, and if there were any layoffs due to the economic fallout from the pandemic, she thought she'd likely be the first to go. Uncertain as she was whether each day would be her last, she was having difficulty concentrating on her work. If her worrying continued to affect her job performance, she was even more likely to be laid off.

We don't think of worry as a strategy because we're not consciously choosing it. Fight-or-flight alarms hijack us well before we're aware it has happened. But worry is a strategy, like panic-shopping and compulsive checking, because it has a clear purpose: get rid of anxiety by eliminating uncertainty. My client's anxiety about whether she'd be laid off was a limbic system alert, *Woo-woo-woo!! DO something!!* —the monkey's call to action. Obsessing over this uncertainty was doing something; it was confirming that uncertainty is a threat. She was feeding the monkey, meaning the only certainty she would get would be the certainty of more anxiety in the future.

To break this anxiety/worry cycle, my client first had to make an intention to allow for the possibility of losing her job. That doesn't mean she wouldn't try to do what she could to reduce that possibility, only that she recognized that no matter how hard or well she worked, uncertainty was, and always would be, present. Having set this intention (Strategy #1) to accept what was beyond her control, she was ready move forward to Strategy #2, curbing her urge to worry about what she couldn't control.

What is so tricky about worry is that it can look like problem-solving. Both are mental activities centered on an uncertainty. The difference is that problem-solving requires the frontal cortex — the part of the brain that performs executive functions, like logical comparison and risk assessment — to be engaged. When our executive brain is disabled by fight-or-flight cocktails, it can't do its job properly. When we are hijacked by the monkey mind, all we can do is worry. To reboot our executive brain, I recommend the following *Five step action plan.*

1. Identify the problem.
2. Brainstorm four possible actions to solve it.
3. Review short-term and long-term consequences of each action.
4. Choose the best action and do it.
5. (Afterward) Evaluate how it worked. Whether it solved the problem or not, pat yourself on the back for doing the exercise!

We'll go into more detail with this action plan in chapter five. Remember that whatever action you choose to take won't necessarily solve the problem. You're doing what you can and allowing the uncertainty to exist. My client decided to take an online course learning a new computer language that would make her less dispensable at her present job, and more qualified should she need to apply for a new job. Acting on what is within our control is a lot healthier than worrying about what isn't within our control.

After this exercise, when my client felt anxious about losing her job again, she engaged Strategy #3, allowing space for the feeling to run its course. She found that when she stopped everything she was doing and allowed her body to process the possible loss of her job, the feeling didn't last for long. And when it came back and she found herself worrying again, she could remind herself of her new expansive strategy. When an old worry reappears, say the words out loud: *Thank you, monkey! I have a plan for this!*

We all need to program our limbic system to adjust to the new uncertainties of the economy. When we are caught up in worry about bills that are due, an unemployment check that hasn't arrived, or any other financial insecurity, remember that we can address problems and assess risk so much better when we're not hijacked by fear.

Treat worry as an opportunity to exercise your three expansive strategies. While we can never be certain we are financially secure, what will better optimize our chances of meeting our financial obligations -- worrying about the problem? ... or identifying actions to take to address it?

Acting on what is within our control is a lot healthier than worrying about what isn't within our control.

Accepting Risk

To be clear, there is nothing wrong with buying toilet paper, taking our temperature, and thinking about our finances; these behaviors are necessary to our survival and well-being. They become certainty-seeking strategies when they are done compulsively in response to urges. Then these necessary behaviors become panic shopping, compulsive checking, or worrying. We engage in dozens, even hundreds of unconscious behaviors aimed at certainty every day. Though individually harmless, collectively they form a behavior pattern that feeds the monkey, making us more and more anxious and doing little to make us safer or improve our well-being. The safety and certainty-oriented behaviors most common in our present crisis — compulsive checking, panic shopping, and worrying — create an entire belief system that dictates, *Before I relax, I must be 100% certain I am safe.*

The folly of this *I-must-be-certain* mind-set is that we can never be certain of anything. Even if the coronavirus disappeared tomorrow, sickness and death would still happen. We were at risk before this pandemic, and we will be after it has passed. And we are quite comfortable taking many of those risks. Every time we sit behind the wheel of a car, we are trusting our own reflexes and judgments to maneuver a two-ton object traveling at high speeds, as well as the reflexes and judgments of hundreds of other drivers whose mistakes could injure or kill us in an instant. Yet "going for a drive" is generally considered a fun activity, one we miss when we are following instructions to limit unnecessary travel.

We can drive without anxiety because we've taken reasonable

Reasonable precaution enables reasonable risk.

precautions: respecting speed limits, stopping at traffic lights, wearing seat belts, driving cars engineered with air bags and crumple zones. Yes, there is still the risk of accident but we view it as a reasonable price to pay for mobility. Reasonable precaution enables reasonable risk.

Driving is one example of an exception to the *I-must-be-certain* mind-set, proof that we can train the monkey to let us relax even when we are not 100% safe. And that's a good thing because a relaxed driver is a safer driver, just as we are safer from the pandemic and financial losses when we can relax enough to think clearly and take wise action.

In a world of rising uncertainty, it seems reasonable to increase our capacity to <u>tolerate</u> uncertainty. Whatever your worry, reframing it as an opportunity to expand, rather than contract, can bring about transformation. Think of a situation that has you worried right now, something that despite your best efforts, could end badly. Assuming you've taken all reasonable precautions, which is a more realistic strategy moving forward -- to continue to spin your wheels trying to eliminate the risk of a bad outcome ... or develop the ability to tolerate that risk?

4. Social Uncertainty

The other day I was on my daily walk on a path that many others use for exercise. I was wearing my face mask when something in the wind tickled my nose. I sneezed loudly, three times in succession. When the sensation passed, I looked around anxiously to see whether other walkers were looking at me with disapproval. Would they think I was sick and contagious, that I shouldn't be out in public? You may recognize this feeling of being in a social spotlight and being judged. The rules around our social behavior are changing so fast we may be constantly asking ourselves *Am I doing this right?*

None of us likes to be judged or criticized. Humans are like pack animals — dependent on each other for survival — and we all share a core fear of being kicked out of the tribe. With its perpetual need for certainty, the monkey mind-set is *If I always do the right thing, I won't be rejected by others.* But with the current rules and recommendations changing daily, and the fact that each of us has our own level of risk tolerance, it is more impossible than ever to secure the guarantee of approval from others.

A client of mine, a mother of two, was in a quandary. Her in-laws, who lived nearby, wanted to continue to visit their grandchildren despite their advanced age and a county shelter-in-place restriction. Although my client loved her mother- and father in-law, she didn't want them to visit; they might expose her kids to the coronavirus. But if she didn't allow them to visit they may get angry, which would strain the relationship. Uncertain what was the right thing to do, she postponed telling them how she felt, and lost sleep worrying about what would happen when she did.

Well-intentioned people will disagree about what to do in this, or any situation. The concept of the "right" or "best" action is another example of how we are blinded by our *must-be-certain* mind-set. Since my client could not be sure of the fallout from denying her in-laws visits with their grandchildren for the duration of the lockdown, she had a great opportunity to practice tolerating uncertainty and build some resilience to anxiety.

She started with Strategy #1 and set an intention to accept whatever reaction her in-laws might have. Strategy #2 was to curb her urge to delay and tell them what her limits were. Strategy #3 was to open to the anxiety she felt, and other emotions, like guilt and shame, that might arise if her in-laws reacted angrily.

Whether you feel ashamed for sneezing in public, or setting a boundary that hurts a loved one, remember that we can never be certain that we are doing it right. All you can be is your authentic self and live with the outcome. And which will give your life more meaning -- the approval of others in one situation? ... or personal authenticity in all situations?

Blaming doesn't keep us safe

A few days ago, I was in a hardware store and needed an employee's assistance finding a part I wanted to buy. As he approached me I saw that he was not wearing a mask, and I could feel my apprehension rise. Then, while I was describing what I was looking for, he wiped his nose with the back of his hand. *Uck!*

It turned out I didn't have all the information on the part I needed. While I looked it up on my phone, I saw out of the corner of my eye that he was rubbing his eyes and touching his face. When I had trouble finding it online, he offered to do it for me, and even reached out to take my phone. "No, I got it," I said firmly, and muddled on until I located it. What a relief it was to get out of that store!

As lockdowns are eased and we venture out to stores, parks and public spaces, we know that others may still be carrying a highly contagious, deadly virus. We expect, or at least hope, that everyone we meet will follow the same safety precautions we do. But of course, not everybody will.

From the perspective of our limbic system, somebody touching their face and shared surfaces is a possible threat. When we can't know for certain that someone is not contagious, the monkey mind assumes they are, which means fight-or-flight alarms for us. Depending on the situation, we can interpret these alarms in lots of different ways, ranging from disgust to anger.

It's very easy for us to direct shame and blame when we're afraid. And the question we must ask is, *Do our judgments of the actions of others protect us?*

Judging, blaming and venting anger at what we perceive as careless or selfish behavior doesn't lower our vulnerability to contagion or assure our well-being. What these behaviors do accomplish is show

Judging, blaming and venting anger at what we perceive as careless or selfish behavior doesn't lower our vulnerability to contagion or assure our well-being

the limbic system that we are "doing something" about the threat, which may give us a little relief. Temporary relief. But since judging, blaming and venting confirm the threat of the others' behavior, they feed the monkey, training it to be even more reactive next time somebody walks too close or touches their face.

What we want is just the opposite — for our limbic system to adjust to the reality that people are not all going to adhere to the same safety standards, and that some risk in our social interactions is inevitable, and not cause for alarm. Setting boundaries is best done with respect and equanimity, not aggression.

A head start

My husband Doug was walking along a local hike-and-bike path one day a few weeks into the pandemic, observing social distancing by staying to one side of the ten-foot-wide path, when a woman approaching from the other direction suddenly started waving at him to move farther away, off to the side of the path. "Get back!" she barked. Instinctively, he complied, but immediately after she passed, he frowned, shook his head angrily, and said to himself, "That's just crazy!"

But when he recounted the incident to me later, he said, "OK, she wasn't crazy. She was just afraid, especially perhaps because I wasn't wearing a mask. And my reaction was fear too. Fear that I wasn't behaving properly, which I didn't want to think about myself. We're all so afraid right now."

Since the pandemic arrived, our limbic system is firing up more frequently and with more urgency. When we're surprised by something we didn't expect, the monkey's *Woo-woo-woo!* can throw us off our ground. We can become defensive, judgmental, even aggressive in an instant. How do we exercise our three expansive strategies when we get slammed so quickly, and with so much fight-or-flight response that our executive functions get hijacked?

Fight-or-flight alarms are the superpower of the limbic system; they hit our nervous system at the speed of light. To challenge the monkey in a race for our experience, especially with the heightened

 uncertainty we face right now, we need a head start. This means that even when we are just going out for a walk,

we would be wise to anticipate some of the things that may trigger our limbic system.

In Doug's case, he headed down the trail unprepared for another hiker who needed more social distancing space to feel comfortable. When she expressed that need aggressively, Doug was overwhelmed, capable only of judgement and resentment in that moment. But his experience can help him get ready for the next time he's hijacked by the monkey.

Training the monkey

To claim any situation as a training opportunity, all we need do is prepare ourselves with a goal and be ready to exercise our three expansive strategies. As stores, restaurants and public spaces open and restrictions are eased, for example, we can remind ourselves that everyone has different needs for social distance and every venue will have different safety rules. You may trigger someone else by your proximity or behavior, or they may trigger you. Ask yourself what values you want to feed on your next trip downtown. How about compassion and equanimity?

Whether you're most anxious about uncertain food supplies, scary body sensations, news events, friends and family connections, or social frictions, remember that you're always accompanied by a security guard with a hair trigger reaction to uncertainty. Unless you get a good head start on the monkey, you'll always be a step behind — reacting rather than acting. In the next chapter, I will introduce seven practices especially suited for our present crisis. Each practice is designed to help you get more comfortable with the uncertainty we face today, and build immunity to anxiety. While these practices may not be appropriate for everyone, I hope some will resonate with you.

5. The Five-Step Action Plan

During this crisis, we worry about real concerns like getting sick, paying our rent or mortgage, unemployment, stock markets plunging, and social isolation. Worry is an attempt to eliminate the threat and put an end to uncertainty. The mindset that fuels worry is *Until I am certain I am safe, I cannot stop worrying.*

There are two problems with this. First, as we have established, we cannot eliminate uncertainty, and our attempts to do so keep us trapped in an endless loop of worry, making us physically and mentally exhausted. Second, worry is about thinking things over and over again, without steps towards making an action plan to address the real concerns we are faced with. The time and energy spent worrying is unproductive.

The 5 Step Action plan addresses both these problems. To illustrate how it works I will use my client Sam, who is in remission from cancer. She lives alone, and because she is immunocompromised she worries about being exposed while shopping for groceries.

1. Cleary define the problem

   I am worried that I will be exposed to the virus when grocery shopping.

2. Brainstorm four possible actions to address this.

   I could use an online delivery service.

   I could be extra careful while shopping for food.

   I could have friends or neighbors do shopping for me.

   I could live on beans and rice so that I would not need to go out for groceries often.

3. Review each possible action for pros and cons.

   A delivery service would limit my exposure, but it is more expensive and I have a fixed income.

   I could do my own shopping and I like that, but I can't control other shoppers and would worry about my exposure to them.

   I could ask friends and neighbors; this would be a safe option, but I don't like to burden others.

   On a rice and bean diet I wouldn't need to go out much, but I would get bored eating the same thing and I'd would miss fresh fruits and vegetables.

38

4. Choose the best action to take.

I can mix and match. I'll do an online delivery once a month to keep my costs down and just ask friends to get me fresh produce.

5. Evaluate how your plan works.

After one month, I will review how things are going financially, and ask my friends how they are feeling about helping me with some of the shopping.

#1 Set an Intention

The 5 Step Action plan moves worry from the low brain, amygdala, where the monkey mind resides, to the higher brain, prefrontal cortex, where we can tap into creativity and constructive planning. None of the options Sam came up with eliminate the possibility that she will be exposed to the virus, but this was not her goal. Her expansive mindset is *Instead of worrying, I'll make a plan.*

#2 Curb the Urge

As we know, there is no plan we can make that will guarantee a perfect outcome. Uncertainty shadows us always, and our limbic system will sound the alarm again and again. Each time you notice you've slipped back into worrying, review your action plan again. Thank the monkey and return to what you were doing before you were hijacked. That's all you can do right now.

#3 Let Fear Metabolize

Of course, the monkey doesn't like to be ignored. When you fail to resume your worrying, you're no longer "doing something" about the problem, so you can expect anxiety, overwhelm, helplessness, or another fight-or-flight based emotion. In Sam's case, she didn't want to be a burden to her friends. This uncomfortable feeling is not a sign that anything is wrong. Difficult feelings are a normal limbic system response to what it perceives as your reckless lack of risk prevention. There is nothing you need to do except welcome whatever feeling arrives.

> *Check in with your body. What sensations are you aware of right now? Bring your attention to your shoulders, gently roll your shoulders, letting go of any unnecessary holding. Come home to your breath, breathing in and breathing out. Try counting to ten breaths, counting each inhale and exhale cycle as one breath. While doing this, you may lose count and be swept away by your habit of thinking or worrying. This is not a problem. Notice how this thought made you feel and simply start over, counting your first inhale and exhale as one. Every time you bring your attention back to your breath you are letting go of needing to be certain, and training yourself to be here and now.*

40

You can download an audio version of this guided meditation at monkeymindbooks.com.

The Long-term Rewards

The 5-step action plan, like all the practices, is the opposite of a quick fix. Don't be disappointed if it doesn't reduce your worrying. This is one phase of an ongoing project: creating a cycle of expanding wise action.

6. Schedule News-feeding

During this pandemic, more than ever, there is constant breaking news. Where the new hotspots of infection are, what safety measures we are advised and ordered to follow, what doctors and scientists are learning about treatment and prevention, not to mention political developments and stock market fluctuations. As good citizens, we need to stay abreast.

But while news informs, it also aims for high ratings, and we pay more attention to things that stimulate our limbic system. As the saying goes, "If it bleeds it leads." Gruesome descriptions and images of bodies being forklifted into freezer trucks, lines of people competing for food and household items, and steep drops in the stock market are headline material; reflective, contextual news reporting is often buried or ignored.

This bias toward the sensational, coupled with our use of notifications, creates a sense of urgency that panders to the monkey mind. Hijacked again and again, every time we check the news we adopt the monkey mind-set: *To be safe, I must know what is happening now.*

It is important to keep informed during this pandemic, but frequent checking of newsfeeds gives us no added benefit and it costs by making us more anxious and stressed. It also creates a dependence -- the more we check, the more urgently we <u>want</u> to check.

Do this practice every day.

#1 Set an Intention

Begin by asking yourself what time-sensitive news, if any, you need to monitor for your business, your health, or your safety. For most of us, there won't be any news source we need to check repeatedly throughout the day.

Since we don't need to know what's happening out there in any given moment, it follows that we don't need to check on what's happening

44

out there in any given moment. Our intention will be to limit the number of times we check and the duration of time we spend checking the news. This will be a different equation for each of us. Estimate how many times a day you are checking the news in one way or another. If you can't make a good assessment, take a day to observe yourself in action, counting the times you check, as well as how much time you spend when you check. Armed with this information, you're ready to set some clear behavioral guidelines.

Choose a specific time, or times, during the day when you'll tune in and catch up. You might pattern it after mealtimes, morning, noon and evening. Or maybe just once a day with the morning paper or the 7 o'clock news hour. For obvious reasons, don't schedule any news feeding within an hour or two of bedtime. Once you've set your scheduled time(s), decide how much you would like to decrease your time spent on news. I suggest you try cutting it in half.

Now, put your commitment into a statement of intention you can remember and remind yourself of throughout the day; for example, *Watching an hour of news in the evening is all I need to stay reasonably informed.*

#2 Curb the Urge

While the newsworthy events in the world are beyond our control, we can control our behavior regarding to them. If we want to have less anxiety about what is happening in the world, we must condition our limbic system to decrease fight-or-flight prompts to check. Visual or audio alerts are especially triggering for our hypersensitive monkey mind. The most impactful way to reduce urges to check is to simply turn off any breaking news notifications you have on your devices.

Once you commit to your schedule, every time you get an urge to check the news, whether by turning on the TV, picking up your phone, or looking at a newspaper, remind yourself of your new intention — *I don't need to know right now* — and return to whatever task or activity you were doing when the urge appeared. If the urge continues, it's time for our third expansive strategy.

#3 Let Fear Metabolize

If you've been checking the news a lot, reducing your checking is going to feel uncomfortable at first. If you've ever had to cut back on your coffee intake, or some other habit, you'll know what to expect. This discomfort is normal and doesn't mean anything is wrong. Remind yourself again of your intention and the long-term goal you are after. Then open to your discomfort in whatever form it takes. To enhance your body's ability to metabolize emotion during this, or any exercise, here is a guided meditation.

5-Minute Progressive Relaxation Practice

Make sure to turn off any notifications while doing this 5-minute relaxation practice. Sit or lie down in a comfortable position. Do a body scan, noticing any areas in your body that you feel are tense. Starting at the top of your head, slowly bring your attention to your forehead, your jaw, your throat, your shoulders, your arms and hands, your chest and upper back, your stomach, your hips, thighs all the way down to your feet. Good. Now tighten your jaw and clench your teeth. Continue to breathe normally while you hold this tension to the count of three, noticing the sensations as you do so. Take a deep breath in, then as you exhale, release the tension in your jaw. Notice how your jaw feels as the tension drains away. Now tighten your shoulders, bringing them up toward your ears. Continue to breathe, and hold the tension in your neck and upper back for a count of three. 1, 2, 3. Now take a big breath in, and as you breathe out, let go of the tension, allowing your shoulders to drop back down. Good. Next, bring your attention to your belly. Suck in your belly button towards your spine, feeling the tension in your ribs, back and belly. Hold it to the count of three. 1, 2, 3. Now take a big breath in, and as you breathe out let your belly relax and soften. Next, make a fist with both of your hands, feeling the tension in your wrists and forearms. Hold the tension while you breathe normally for a count of three. 1,2,3. Now take a big breath in, and as you breathe out, let your hands relax. Notice the difference between tensing and releasing. With each release, we expand our tolerance for our uncertainty about what's happening in the news, and increase our appreciation for what's happening here and now.

You can download an audio version of this guided meditation at monkeymindbooks.com.

When you turn off your news notifications, consider turning on a periodic notification to do this 5-minute relaxation practice. Tensing and releasing our muscles overrides the limbic system and activates the rest-and-digest response in our nervous system. With a relaxed state of body and mind, we can best meet the challenges we face in uncertain times.

The Long-term Rewards

Every time you resist an urge to check the news, you are training the monkey mind that you are in charge of staying informed, not it. Repeated training will mean fewer fight-or-flight alarms throughout the day, less stress, and greater ability to stay present with what is happening right here, right now. Sometimes, a little more ignorance is, indeed, bliss!

7. Be All Right, Even if You're Wrong

No matter what safety precautions we take when interacting with others, be they strangers, friends, neighbors, relatives or family members, it's impossible to make everyone happy. Because we all have different ideas about what is safe, no matter what you do, you're bound to upset others. But nothing short of pleasing everybody will do for our limbic system. If you get a critical look, the monkey will howl, *Woo-woo-woo!! You blew it!* When we're hijacked by the monkey, we think, *If I'm criticized, it means I've done something wrong.*

#1 Set an Intention

Before we expose ourselves to the next social situation, choose an alternative to this monkey mind-set. For example, you could say *If I displease anyone, I can forgive myself, whether they forgive me or not*. This expansive strategy sets a wider stage for you to play in, where the risk of others' judgments won't limit your experience.

#2 Curb the Urge

Fear that others may disapprove of our actions will spark a variety of urges. First, we may edit our behavior in anticipation of disappointing someone, like the mother who postponed setting social-distancing limits with her in-laws. If we suspect we're doing something wrong, such as not standing in line at the proper spot, we may ask others for reassurance. We may even have the urge to complain about the people we think are judging us by judging them back. (There's another practice for this one.) All these behaviors are subtle forms of attempting to gain certainty that we are doing the right thing, and thus feeding the monkey to make us more anxious in the future. By interrupting these urges, we train the monkey that doing the best we can in these trying times is enough. There is no need to sound the alarm.

#3 Let Fear Metabolize

We all want to be accepted and respected and to feel a sense of belonging. When our social connections are stressed by the additional demands of social distancing, we are likely to experience fear, embarrassment, shame, or insecurity. We want to greet these emotions with unconditional acceptance and kindness. Since self-compassion doesn't come naturally to many of us, I suggest you prepare yourself with this imaginal exercise. It will serve as a rehearsal for the real experience of being judged or criticized.

Imagine a situation where you felt someone judged you for your behavior. Perhaps you made a social distancing mistake and you experienced a sense of shame, embarrassment or guilt. Or you can imagine a situation that may occur in the future. Picture as much detail as you can— where you are, who you are with, the expression on the person's face who is upset with you, even the words they are saying.

Now notice how this memory or image makes you feel. Being judged activates fear about losing connection. Where do you feel this fear? You may feel heat in your face, tightening in your jaw, your heart may beat faster or you may feel contraction in your chest. These uncomfortable feelings are not a sign that you did anything wrong. You are doing the best that you can. It is impossible to please everyone. Right now, you don't need to fix anything.

Allow yourself to feel exactly as you are feeling. Breathe into the part of your body where you feel the most discomfort. As you breathe in, open and soften; as you breathe out, let go. Breathe in, allowing yourself to feel whatever is coming up. Breathe out, letting go of self judgement.

The next time someone judges you, or you think they may be judging you, practice accepting the situation and yourself. Your limbic system will be activated, and when this happens, remind yourself that it is okay to feel whatever you are experiencing, and remember to breathe.

You can download an audio version of this guided meditation at monkeymindbooks.com.

Long-term Rewards

Learning to be resilient to our anxiety about the possible judgments of others not only allows us to be more honest and authentic; it will ultimately give us the courage to stand up for ourselves should judgements occur.

8. Forgive in Advance

As sheltering in place is loosened, we will have more contact with one another. While most of us will welcome social contact, there will be ample opportunity for uncertainty and anxiety. The virus is still with us, and everyone whose paths we cross may be a carrier. While there are rules and recommendations, as human beings we have a wide variety of responses. Some of us will be more stringent with safety precautions, and others will be looser. The stakes are high, and we are dependent upon others for our health and well-being. When someone is not being as scrupulous as we would like, we will suffer limbic alarms. The monkey mind-set is *Unless I am certain others are following the rules I am not safe.* This way of thinking makes us want to identify and correct others' transgressions. The one thing we can be certain of is that people are bound to disappoint, irritate and anger us.

#1 Set an Intention

Since we know in advance that people will not always behave as we'd like them to, let's prepare ourselves with an intention that will allow us to do our business in the world without needing them to behave as we'd like them to. Our new mindset is *I cannot control other people's behavior, and I can cope with the uncertainty that causes.* When we expect and accept this, we are more relaxed and less reactive in the moment. If we need to set a boundary with someone, we will be more respectful, and if we need to retreat and distance ourselves, we can do so with more grace.

#2 Curb the Urge

When someone brushes by us too closely, or isn't wearing a mask in a situation where we think they should, or appears to be hoarding something we may need in the future, the most common urge we have is to judge. We may feel compelled to correct them openly, but more likely we will want to replay the offense in our minds or retell the story to those who will join us in the blame game. Our job is to notice these urges before we act on them, if possible. If we catch ourselves acting on an urge, that's good too. Wherever we interrupt the cycle is great.

#3 Let Fear Metabolize

With this practice, we can expect to notice irritation, disgust, and anger. The common denominator for these feelings is fear -- fear that we'll be exposed to the virus or fear that we won't have enough food and supplies. To have compassion for the perceived failings of others, we'll need to have compassion for our own discomfort first. Open with kindness to whatever you're feeling.

To help face real life situations you may encounter, start by imagining situations from the past or that could happen in the future to be better prepared.

Imagine being out in public and another person doing something that you believe is unsafe or insensitive. They may not have on a mask, they may be touching their face and then objects that others may touch, they may be stockpiling things that are in short supply. As you bring this scenario to mind, notice what is happening in your body. Where are you noticing contraction? In your jaw, your throat, your shoulders, your hands, your chest, your stomach? When we feel threatened by other people's behavior, it is normal to feel anxious and angry. Instead of judging or lashing out, allow yourself to feel this contraction. Now exaggerate the contraction in your body: clench your teeth tightly, continue to breath normally as you feel the contraction in your jaw, take a big breath in, and breath out, soften your jaw, let the tension drain from your face. Now make fists with your hands, clench your hands tightly, feel the tension in your fingers, palms, forearms, continue to breath as you hold this tension, now a big breath in, and as you breathe out relax your hands, let them soften. Notice the difference between tensing and releasing. Tense your belly, bring your belly button in toward your spine, feel the tension in your belly, ribs, low back, now take a big breath in, as you breath out, let your belly relax and soften.

Once again, bring to mind another person doing something you think is unsafe, try to imagine this, but keep your body more relaxed, open. If you notice tightening up again, exaggerate the tension in this part of your body, then breath in and let go.

You can download an audio version of this guided meditation at monkeymindbooks.com.

We do not have control over other people's actions. As restrictions change, we will be exposed to more situations where we feel upset. When we anticipate this, it is easier to accept it. When we accept it, we are less reactive and can take wiser action. The next time you go out, notice when you get triggered, and once you notice this, tense and release your hands, your jaw, or your belly. If you need to take action by moving away or requesting that someone else change their behavior, see if you can do it with gentleness.

Long-term Rewards

Trusting that we are safe enough, when we can't be certain we are, is hard work. Resisting our tendency to blame others for our discomfort is a new trick. Remember that with practice we develop skills we don't yet have. And there is no greater skill than compassion.

9. Sensation or Symptom? Let it Be

Among the symptoms of Covid-19 published by the CDC are muscle pain, headache, and sore throat. Who hasn't experienced these recently? Since we can't be certain that a sensation is not a symptom of Covid-19, our limbic system may trigger repeated fight-or-flight alarms, causing us increased anxiety and provoking more checking and worry behaviors. When we find ourselves obsessing over a scratchy throat, taking our temperature repeatedly, looking up symptoms on the internet and/or calling or emailing our doctors repeatedly, we can know we've been hijacked with the monkey's mind-set: *I need to be 100% certain that I am not sick with the Coronavirus.*

#1 Set an Intention

The key to feeling less stressed is to tolerate our uncertainty about the random sensations our bodies generate. The expansive intention we want to have is *Unless this condition persists, or is accompanied by others, I'll assume it's not a symptom of the coronavirus."*

#2 Curb the Urge

We'll begin our curb-the-urge strategy by monitoring what sensations we are fixating on and what behaviors we engage in response to them. Here's an example of what that might look like.

Checking for Symptoms Chart

Day/Date	Sensation	Behavior	# times
wednesday	sore throat	look at throat w/flashlight	3
		felt for swollen glands	4
	felt hot	felt forehead	3
		took temperature	1
thursday		Asked partner to feel forehead	1
	headache	looked up on internet	2
		called doctor	1

You can download a blank chart to help you keep track at monkeymindbooks.com.

Next, we will restrict the number of times we give in to the urge to check to see if we might be sick. For example, if you take your temperature multiple times a day, you could restrict it to once a day. Or if, you are feeling brave, make it once or twice a week. Each time you curb the urge to check, remind yourself of your expansive intention.

#3 Let Fear Metabolize

It is normal to feel anxious and confused when we're uncertain, especially uncertain about our bodily health. As an alternative to worrying and checking to eliminate the uncertainty, allow yourself to feel exactly as you are feeling right now.

> *Bring your attention to the part of your body where you notice the sensation ... and breathe into this part of your body. Imagine that your breath is expanding space, making room for whatever you are feelings or sensations are there. Instead of bracing against the feeling, allow yourself to soften. Soften your jaw, soften your hands, soften your belly.*

You can download an audio version of this guided meditation at monkeymindbooks.com.

Remember, you are not trying to make the sensation or your anxiety about the sensation go away. You are simply creating an expansive space where your fear can play itself out. Fear has a way of dissipating when we do not contract around it, however you mustn't rush it along. Welcome it so long as it persists.

The Long-term Rewards

As you build resilience to your fear about whether a sensation is a symptom, you are conditioning your limbic system to be less reactive to uncertainty, or to put it another way, training the monkey mind who is boss. Less reactivity to sensations means less unnecessary anxiety and stress, making for a healthier body and mind. The higher values you are feeding with this practice are patience, courage, and wisdom.

10. The Empty Shelf Challenge

When we hear about shortages of supplies that we are accustomed to being plentiful, such as flour and meat, when we see people lined up with carts full of toilet paper, or come across empty shelves in stores, our limbic system is triggered and we get hijacked with

emotion. Our mind-set becomes *"I cannot rest or relax unless I know I will not run out of things."* Strategies like excessive worry and panic-shopping are attempts to eliminate the uncertainty of running out of supplies. We rely on competition rather than cooperation, and when we can't find what we were looking for, we are prone to feelings of defeat and helplessness. The "Empty Shelf Challenge" is a practice that allows for the real existing supply chain uncertainties, and builds resilience to anxiety about that uncertainty.

This can be an ongoing practice you can do every time you go shopping.

#1 Set an Intention

Rather than trying to stockpile supplies during this time of crisis, decide to stockpile flexibility and creativity. Our intention is to accept that not everything we need will be available. The expansive mind-set we will cultivate is *I can cope creatively if I run out of something.* This will foster more cooperation rather than competition with others, and help us to rest and relax despite any shortages that may appear.

#2 Curb the Urge

When you see an empty shelf, or read about a shortage of supplies, instead of trying to find the item elsewhere, think up a creative plan for what you will do without it. When my client could not find flour for chocolate chip cookies, she made rice crispy treats instead. When I imagined running out of toilet paper, I pictured myself panhandling for spare rolls in my town. This made me smile rather than panic, and I felt confident that if I ran out, either someone would share or I'd find a creative substitute.

#3 Let Fear Metabolize

As you walk by an empty shelf, read about a shortage, or see people lining up for something that is in short supply, notice what is happening in your body. You may feel a tightening in your shoulders, your stomach may clench up, your heart may beat faster. You may feel anxiety, panic, anger at the supply chain or at other shoppers who are taking away things you may need or want. Notice what urges this gives rise to. Your job is to allow whatever bodily sensations and emotions you are aware of to be here. Bring your attention to your breath. Breathe in to the count of three. 1,2,3. Breath out to the count of six. 1,2,3,4,5,6. With each in-breath, soften your chest, your belly, and your shoulders. With each out breath, surrender to the feeling of uncertainty. In, 1,2,3, soften. Out, 1,2,3,4,5,6, surrender to uncertainty, In, 1,2,3. Out, 1,2,3,4,5,6.

You can download an audio version of this guided meditation at monkeymindbooks.com.

The Long-term Rewards

While this practice may appear to be about coping without today's empty shelf item, you are building an expansive strategic plan to use again and again. The more flexible and creative you can be without that steak you wanted, the more flexible and creative you will be in finding ways to handle *any* shortage you might face, not only during this crisis, but for the rest of your life.

11. Make Time to Worry

Although we normally think of worry as an intrusive influence on our experience, we can work more efficiently with the problem of worry by treating it as a failed *behavior strategy*. When we engage in worry, we can't be present with other tasks or activities; it requires too much of our attention. And after a worry session, we seldom have anything to show for our efforts. We just can't solve problems very well when we're feeling anxious. Worry is a behavior that doesn't serve us well but, like all behaviors, it can be brought under our control.

To do that we must recognize the real function of worry, which is to insulate us from anxiety about things beyond our control. Running a problem over and over in our minds distracts us from our feelings of fear and helplessness. Unconsciously, we prefer to worry rather than experience these uncomfortable emotions. Our monkey mindset is *I cannot handle feeling uncomfortable.*

To regain control of our worry behavior, first we're going make an executive decision about one aspect of worry that our limbic system usually gets to decide: when to do it. Schedule a time today when you can devote ten minutes to nothing but uninterrupted worry. Yes, I know it sounds really wrong. Trust me, this is an extremely effective practice.

#1 Set an Intention

As you know, our overall intention as outlined in this book is to accept the uncertainty in our lives rather than resist it. For this practice, our specific intention can be expressed as, *I can handle the thoughts and feelings I am having while I think about the uncertainties in my life.* To help yourself zero in on what those uncertainties are, before you begin your self-assigned "worry time," write down your top five worries so you have them for reference. Then set the timer and go. Worry as hard as you can, and allow yourself to feel whatever comes up.

You can schedule worry time for the morning and/or afternoon, but I would not recommend doing it right before bed. You can download a form to use during your regularly scheduled time at monkeymindbooks.com.

#2 Curb the Urge

You can expect that during the 23 hours and 50 minutes of your day that are not scheduled for worrying will bring plenty of opportunities to worry as usual. The monkey mind isn't going to want to play by your rules. When you notice yourself slipping into familiar worry behavior, remind yourself that you have a scheduled time to worry, and now is not that time. You can even write down the specific worry you are having, so that you won't forget about it when it comes to your scheduled worry time. When you postpone worry, you're bossing the monkey. Your expansive strategy is to return to whatever you were doing here and now. Worry can wait.

#3 Let Fear Metabolize

Once you have written down you worries, notice what is happening in your body. Gently scan your body for areas of tension, starting at the top of your head, slowly moving to your forehead, your jaw, your throat, your shoulders, your arms, your hands, your chest, your belly, your buttocks, your thighs, all the way down to your feet. Imagine at your feet there is a welcome mat. You are welcoming in not only your worries, but all the physical sensations and emotions that go along with the things you are uncertain about. It is okay to be feeling exactly as you are feeling right now. You are not alone. Most of us are feeling these same things. It is normal and natural to have feelings of fear, of helplessness, of overwhelm. Let yourself feel these things. Imagine that your feelings are like waves in the ocean, swelling and falling. If you notice that your body is contracting around the feelings, gently open to these feelings, no matter how painful they are. Open your chest by rolling your shoulders and letting them relax down. Soften your belly by breathing into it and making room for what you are feeling right now. Open your hands so that the palms are facing upward, as you surrender to the emotions and physical sensations that are normal and natural to have during times of crisis.

You can download an audio version of this guided meditation at monkeymindbooks.com.

The Long-term Rewards

As we grow more comfortable with the fear that triggers worry, there is less cause for worry, no matter what challenges lay before us.

Epilogue

The Covid-19 pandemic has threatened the lives and welfare of each and every one of us. My hope is that this book will help you to understand that, even in daunting and unpredictable circumstances, you always have the significant choice to either contract or expand.

When we contract, we devote our awareness and energy to an attempt to eliminate the possibility of future loss. But when events are beyond our control, contraction robs us of our presence of mind and body and prolongs our suffering. Expansion, however, increases the possibility of staying fully present with what's happening now, good or bad; it strengthens our tolerance for uncertainty and possible loss; and it sustains our ability to be wise, flexible, creative, resilient, co-operative and compassionate to ourselves and others.

The three strategies set forth in this book — setting an intention to accept uncertainty, curbing urges to attain certainty, and letting fear of uncertainty metabolize — are not only based on modern Cognitive Behavioral Therapy. These strategies were described by the Stoic philosophers of Greece and Rome, and have been practiced throughout the centuries as "skillful means" in many spiritual disciplines. They represent a time-tested, effective response to fear in all its many forms, from terror of impending death to anxiety about a new wrinkle we see in the mirror.

For these strategies to become your default strategy whenever you lose clarity, I suggest you visit the practices in this book again and again. Determined as you are to expand your tolerance for uncertainty and reap the rewards, the monkey mind is a slow learner, and will need lots of training before it begins to relax its grip. But relax it will. As someone who has worked with anxiety of every variety for many years, I am confident that there is nothing unique about how you feel and nothing standing in your way. The future, uncertain as it is, is yours to claim!

Other books by Jennifer Shannon include

Don't Feed the Monkey Mind
How to Stop the Cycle of Anxiety, Worry and Fear

The Monkey Mind Workout for Uncertainty
Break Free of Anxiety and Build Resilience in 30 Days!
(due Dec 2020)

The Anxiety Survival Guide for Teens

The Shyness and Social Anxiety Workbook for Teens

Made in the USA
Monee, IL
04 October 2020